SCIENCE WORKS

THE ROCK FACTORY

THE STORY OF ROCKS AND STONES

IT'S CRYSTAL CLEAR!

Jacqui Bailey Matthew Lilly

A & C BLACK · LONDON

Our story of a stone begins thousands of millions of years ago.

Back then, the surface of the Earth was just red-hot rock, clouds of swirling gases, water — and not much else.

There were no plants or animals. The only things that moved were the wind, water, and rivers of hot rock from exploding volcanoes.

The rivers of rock were escaping from deep inside the Earth — from the rock factory.

Our planet is mostly made of rock, but it isn't solid all the way through. It's made up of different layers, a bit like a soft-boiled egg.

The topmost layer is the crust. This is a thin layer of hard rock, like the shell of an egg. The crust covers the whole of the Earth. The land we live on is part of it, and the oceans lie on top of it.

HMMM, I'M FEELING A LITTLE CRUSTY TODAY!

Underneath the crust is the mantle. This is a very thick layer of immensely hot and heavy rock material — like a thick, stiff cake mix.

The mantle is the rock factory. It's where most of the rock in the crust originally came from, and it's where the stone in our story was made.

Below the mantle is the super-hot core. It has a layer of liquid metal on the outside, and is solid metal on the inside. The core is like an oven at the heart of the Earth, and its heat spreads right up through the mantle.

The mantle is hottest next to the core and grows gradually cooler as it gets closer and closer to the crust.

As the material crept upwards, the heat around it grew a little less, and the weight pressing down from above began to lighten.

ARE WE THERE YET?

HEY IT'S GETTING COOLER!

Crust

Mantle

Core

Eventually it arrived at a special spot — and it began to change …

Rock making is a very slow business. It takes millions and millions of years for rock material to rise from the bottom of the mantle to the top.

Our clump of material had reached just the right place in the mantle for it to turn into a stone!

Most minerals turn into crystals, but only when the pressure (weight pressing on them) and temperature (level of heat) are exactly right for that type of mineral.

How does that happen? Well, it goes something like this.

Rock is made from stuff called minerals. There are lots of different kinds of minerals and they all shift and stir about in the mantle, like the ingredients in a cake mix.

HEY! WHAT'S HAPPENING?

HELP!

As minerals get closer to the crust they begin to cool — and as they cool they harden into special flat-sided shapes called crystals.

Each kind of mineral forms its own type of crystal — and when lots of crystals lock together, they make rocks.

Crystals

Most rocks and stones are made of a mixture of minerals, with crystals of different shapes and sizes.

Granite is a hard, speckled-looking rock made of four kinds of crystals. Each speckle is a different crystal.

Crystals

Granite

HEAR THAT? I'M A SPECIAL STONE.

But our stone was different — its crystals were all the same. They had formed from just one material (called carbon). This made our stone a very special stone.

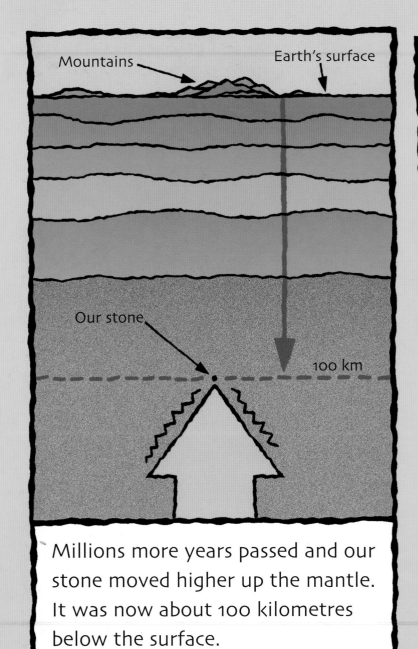

Mountains

Earth's surface

Our stone

100 km

Millions more years passed and our stone moved higher up the mantle. It was now about 100 kilometres below the surface.

Above the stone, the mantle mixture pushed up against the crust. Some of the mixture cooled and hardened, and stuck to the bottom of the crust.

Crust

13

As the rock mixture moves up the mantle, some of it softens and turns to a grainy liquid. This liquid is called magma.

Magma moves more easily through the mantle than the rest of the rock mixture. When it reaches the crust it builds up underneath it. Then it pushes and squeezes its way into any gaps in the crust that it can find.

If it finds a gap it surges into it, tearing a hole right through the crust and gushing onto the surface, like fizzy pop from a shaken bottle.

This is what happens in a volcano.

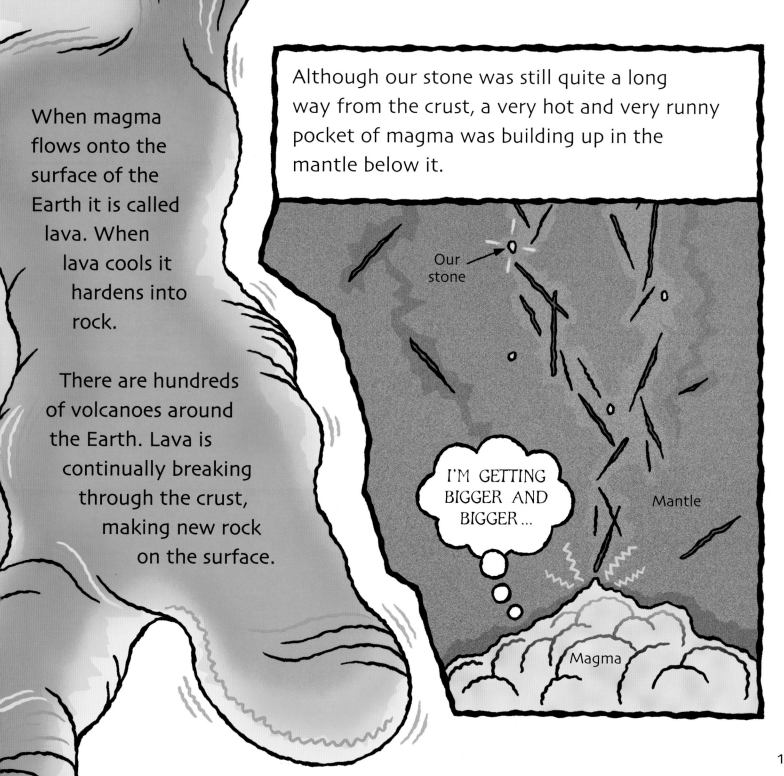

When magma flows onto the surface of the Earth it is called lava. When lava cools it hardens into rock.

There are hundreds of volcanoes around the Earth. Lava is continually breaking through the crust, making new rock on the surface.

Although our stone was still quite a long way from the crust, a very hot and very runny pocket of magma was building up in the mantle below it.

Our stone

I'M GETTING BIGGER AND BIGGER...

Mantle

Magma

The pocket of magma got bigger and bigger and, instead of seeping through the mantle mixture like most magma, it pushed and pushed against it.

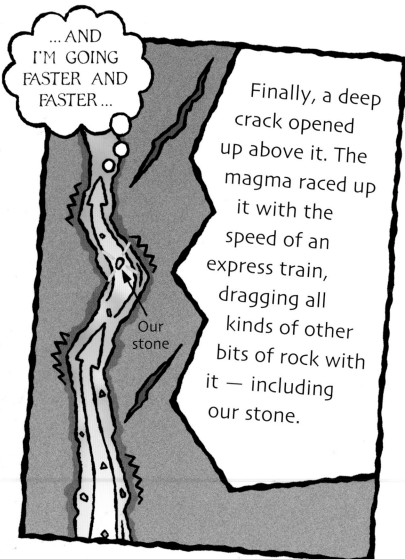

... AND I'M GOING FASTER AND FASTER ...

Our stone

Finally, a deep crack opened up above it. The magma raced up it with the speed of an express train, dragging all kinds of other bits of rock with it — including our stone.

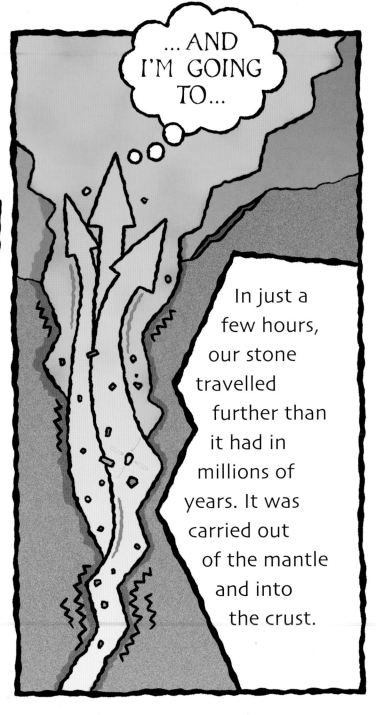

... AND I'M GOING TO ...

In just a few hours, our stone travelled further than it had in millions of years. It was carried out of the mantle and into the crust.

Up above, the first wave of magma reached the surface.

The ground ripped open and a blast of scorching steam and ash exploded into the air, instantly burning up anything it touched.

...EXPLODE!

Lumps of red-hot rock and blobs of lava rained down around the volcano like a gigantic firework — and our stone was brought closer and closer to the surface.

Not many volcanoes are as explosive as this. With some, lava oozes out of the crust slowly, like jam squeezed from a doughnut.

When the explosion ended there was a huge hole in the ground, like a giant ice-cream cone, filled with shattered rocks and cooling magma.

The stone stayed where it was.

our stone

Time passed and on the surface things changed. The bowl-shaped top of the volcano filled with water and made a lake.

Birds and other animals came to drink at the lake, and trees and bushes grew around it.

The wind and weather wore away at the bowl. The lake overflowed and ran down the hillside to join a river far below.

Over millions of years, the ground around the bowl and the rock inside it were broken up into tiny pieces and washed away.

One day, our stone was washed away too. It rolled downhill and into the river.

The stone sat with other stones on the riverbed. Fish nosed around it and sometimes layers of mud covered it.

When animals waded into the water they churned the riverbed around and the stone was rolled from place to place.

One day, a boy came and played by the river. He dug his hands into the riverbed and pulled up a handful of wet, shiny pebbles.

He picked out our stone and looked at it carefully. It wasn't like the other stones. It was muddy and dull but it looked like a piece of glass and he could almost see through it.

MAYBE THIS IS A LUCKY STONE. I THINK I'LL KEEP IT.

The boy put the stone in his pocket and took it home.

When the boy showed the stone to his parents they got very excited. They took it to a jeweller's shop in a nearby town.

HMMM! I WONDER...

WHERE DID YOU FIND THIS?

The jeweller held the stone up to the light and peered at it closely through his eyeglass.

He reached for some tools and tried to scratch the surface of the stone, but he couldn't mark it. Then he measured it, weighed it and wrote down some notes.

At last he looked up. 'You're a very lucky boy,' he said.

DIAMONDS ARE FOREVER

Diamonds are the hardest natural material in the world. They can only be cut by another diamond.

LOOK OUT, EARTH, HERE I COME!

Diamonds are also among the oldest things on Earth. They may be as much as 3 billion years old. But some diamonds are even older than this. They are found in meteorites — chunks of rock that fall to Earth from space. Meteorites can contain tiny bits of diamond up to 5 billion years old.

PHEW!

A COOL CRUST

Scientists think the Earth formed from dust and gas whirling around the Sun about 4.6 billion years ago. It took over a billion years for the Earth to cool down enough for the crust to form and the oceans to fill with water. The crust is much thinner under the oceans than under the land. In some places it is only about 6 kilometres thick. Under land it can be up to 70 kilometres thick.

HOT ROCKS

granite

Most rocks belong to one of three groups. Rocks that are made when magma or lava hardens are called igneous (*ig-nee-us*) or fiery rock. Granite is a type of igneous rock.

Rocks that are heated or squeezed so much they turn into a different sort of rock are called metamorphic (*met-uh-maw-fic*) or changed rock. Marble is a metamorphic rock made from limestone.

marble

Limestone belongs to the third group, known as sedimentary rock. When surface rocks are worn down into tiny pieces and washed into the ocean, they form layers of mud on the ocean floor. Over millions of years the layers pile up, until the ones at the bottom are squeezed into solid rock again.

MIGHTY MINERALS

Minerals don't only make rocks, they help build our bodies, too. Some of the chemicals in minerals, such as calcium, help our bones and teeth to grow properly. We get most of the minerals we need from the food we eat. Farmers often add extra minerals to the soil to grow stronger and healthier plants.

TRY IT AND SEE

GROW YOUR OWN CRYSTALS

Lots of everyday materials are made from crystals. Water forms crystals when it freezes into ice — snowflakes are tiny masses of ice crystals. Salt crystals form when seawater dries up.

Try growing your own crystals. It may take a week or so, but the longer you wait the better the crystals will be.

You will need:
- A measuring jug
- Hot water
- Salt
- A teaspoon
- A wooden spoon
- Food dye (if you have it)
- A glass jar
- A pencil and some wool

 1 Ask an adult to boil some water and pour about 100 ml into the measuring jug.

2 While the water is still hot, add a teaspoon of salt and carefully stir the mixture with the wooden spoon. When the salt has dissolved, add another teaspoonful.

When that has dissolved, add another one. Keep going until the salt stops dissolving and starts to collect in the bottom of the jug — after about four teaspoons.

 3 Stir in a few drops of food dye. This isn't vital, but your crystals will look more interesting.

4

Pour the coloured salt-water into the glass jar.

5 Cut a short length of wool and tie one end to the middle of the pencil. Balance the pencil on top of the jar so that the wool dangles right into the liquid.

6 Put your jar somewhere where it will not be disturbed. Gradually, the water in the jar will cool down and start to evaporate — it will turn to a gas and float into the air.

The remaining water will not be able to hold onto the dissolved salt any longer. The salt will cling to the wool and to the sides of the jar and form crystals.

Once crystals start forming on your wool, try putting it into a fresh batch of salt water (make sure the mixture has cooled first). This encourages the crystals to grow on the wool rather than on the sides of the jar.

ROCKY FACTS

Diamond mining in South Africa began in the 1860s when a 15-year-old boy, Erasmus Jacobs, found 'a pebble' on the bank of a river on his father's farm. It was a large diamond. Today, most of the world's diamonds come from mines in Australia, Africa and Russia.

The deepest hole ever drilled into the Earth was in Russia. It reached just over 12 kilometres down into the crust. After that, the heat and pressure of the rock softened the metal drill so much it could not go any further.

There are about 500 active volcanoes in the world today and lots more that are sleeping or dormant. Volcanoes can be dormant for thousands of years and then suddenly burst into life again.

INDEX

calcium 25

carbon 11

core 7

crust 6, 7, 10, 12, 13, 14, 15, 16, 24

crystals 10, 11, 26-27

diamond mining 28

diamonds 23, 24

Earth 4, 6
    drilling into 28
    formation of 24
    inside 5, 6-7
    surface of 4, 14, 15, 17, 18

gases 4

granite 11, 25

igneous rocks 25

jeweller 22

land 6, 24

lava 15, 17, 25

limestone 25

liquid rock 14

magma 14, 15, 16, 17, 18, 25

mantle 7, 8, 9, 10, 12, 13, 14, 15, 16

marble 25

metal 7

metamorphic rocks 25

meteorites 24

minerals 10, 11, 25

oceans 6, 24, 25

sedimentary rocks 25

volcanoes 5, 14, 15, 17, 18, 28

water 4, 18

weather 19

SOME ROCKY WEBSITES TO VISIT

http://www.bbc.co.uk/schools/scienceclips/ages/7_8/rocks_soils.shtml = test a range of rocks to find out different things about them.

http://www.windows.ucar.edu/tour/link=/earth/geology/geology.html = 'Windows to the Universe' is run by the Michigan University Corporation for Atmospheric Research. It's got great information on rocks, minerals and the Earth. Visit their 'Kid Space', too.

http://www.enchantedlearning.com/subjects/volcano = for good info about volcanoes and lots of other stuff.

For Chris
JB

For Daniel and Lydia
ML

First published in 2006 by
A & C Black Publishers Limited
38 Soho Square London W1D 3HB
www.acblack.com

Created for A & C Black Publishers Limited by

two's COMPANY

Copyright © Two's Company 2006

ISBN-10: 0-7136-7355-9 (hbk)
ISBN-13: 978-0-713-67355-5 (hbk)
ISBN-10: 0-7136-7356-7 (pbk)
ISBN-13: 978-0-713-67356-2 (pbk)

Printed and bound in China by Leo Paper Products

A & C Black uses paper produced with elemental chlorine-free
pulp, harvested from managed sustainable forests.

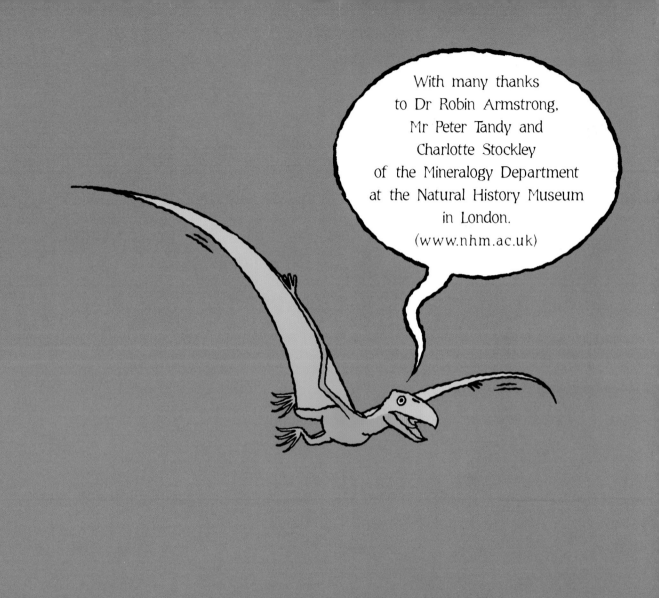

With many thanks
to Dr Robin Armstrong,
Mr Peter Tandy and
Charlotte Stockley
of the Mineralogy Department
at the Natural History Museum
in London.
(www.nhm.ac.uk)